E.M

RADE...
SHREWSBUR...
SY3 9BJ

SMDS
MADELEY COURT SCHOOL
COURT STREET, MADELEY
TELFORD TF7 5DZ
Telephone: 585704

Let's Discuss
HOMELESSNESS

Ann Kramer

Let's Discuss

Let's Discuss Abortion
Let's Discuss AIDS
Let's Discuss Animal Rights
Let's Discuss Disability
Let's Discuss Drinking
Let's Discuss Drugs
Let's Discuss Education
Let's Discuss Family Life
Let's Discuss Health and Fitness
Let's Discuss Homelessness
Let's Discuss Law and Order
Let's Discuss the Media

Let's Discuss Old Age
Let's Discuss Pollution
Let's Discuss Pop Music
Let's Discuss Poverty
Let's Discuss Racism
Let's Discuss Religion
Let's Discuss Sex
Let's Discuss Smoking
Let's Discuss Unemployment
Let's Discuss Violence
Let's Discuss Women's Rights

First published in 1989 by
Wayland (Publishers) Limited
61 Western Road, Hove
East Sussex BN3 1JD, England

Editor: William Wharfe
Consultant: Jackie Brock,
  Information and Training Adviser,
  Hammersmith and Fulham Housing Aid Services
Designer: Ross George

British Library Cataloguing in Publication Data

Kramer, Ann *1946–*
  Let's discuss homelessness.
  1. England. Homelessness
  I. Title II. Series
  363.5'1

ISBN 1-85210-440-6

© Copyright 1989
Wayland (Publishers) Limited

Typeset, printed and bound
in the UK at The Bath Press, Avon

Front cover: *Unemployed and homeless – nothing to do and nowhere to go until the shelter opens at 10pm. Many young people find themselves in this situation when they move to a city.*

Contents

Introduction	4
Defining Homelessness	9
Case Study 1: Bill, aged 43	11
Who are the Homeless?	13
Case Study 2: Mary, aged 22	17
Housing in the UK	19
Case Study 3: Maggie, aged 78	28
Young and Homeless	30
Case Study 4: Rose, aged 19	37
Tackling Homelessness	39
Useful Addresses	45
Glossary	46
Further Reading	47
Index	48

The case studies in this book are fictitious. They are not subject to copyright and may be reproduced for use in the classroom.

Introduction

The 1980s have seen a growing concern with the overall housing situation in Britain. Respected public figures such as Lord Scarman (the UK President of the 1987 International Year of Shelter for the Homeless), local government bodies and charities (such as Shelter and Crisis at Christmas) all argue that we are facing a new housing crisis that needs to be addressed immediately.

As proof of this they point to the rising number of homeless people. In 1979, local authorities accepted a duty to offer permanent accommodation to 53,000 households—mainly families, pensioners and people with a physical disability or a learning disability. In 1987, this had doubled to 103,000 households. These statistics produced by the Department of the Environment do not include single people or couples without children. So they do not completely cover the number of people seeking permanent accommodation. The number of homeless people—those without a roof over their head and those unsatisfactorily housed who are seeking a permanent home elsewhere—has never been so high.

In some inner-city areas, such as here in Toxteth, Liverpool, the poor standard of housing has become a major issue.

If people cannot afford to maintain their property, problems such as damp can become so bad as to make their homes uninhabitable.

Some people become homeless because their old homes have ceased to be habitable. The number of homes in Britain in need of repair is spiralling. Government statistics produced in 1983 showed that over half a million properties needed repairs costing over £7,000, and a further quarter of a million needed repairs costing between £2,300 and £7,000. Over one million dwellings were considered unfit for human habitation, and there were 1,200,000 households needing rehousing, many because their privately-rented homes were unsuitable.

Investment in local authority (council) housing has fallen dramatically. In 1979, £1,800 million was invested in building and repairing local authority dwellings; by 1987, this had fallen to just over £400 million, a decline of over 75 per cent. Some people criticize the present government for allowing this to happen. However, the government points out that there has been a long-term improvement in British housing conditions. In 1951, 9.7 million households were regarded as living in unsatisfactory conditions: for example, lacking an inside toilet, or in overcrowded dwellings. By 1983, this number had dropped to approximately 2 million. Since 1945, over 8 million dwellings have been added to the housing stock in England and Wales and 1.5 million unfit dwellings have been demolished. The government also points out that more people are able to choose to buy their own homes. Since 1945, home ownership has more than doubled and now accounts for around 65 per cent of accommodation in England and Wales (although only 33 per cent in Scotland).

Overall, housing conditions may have improved over the last 40 years, but this is little comfort to those who are homeless today, or who are living in unsatisfactory accommodation.

Of course, Britain is not alone in having problems in housing people adequately. More than one quarter of the world's population lives in inadequate shelters. In the Indian city of Bombay, more than 100,000 people

In Bombay, India, there is a sharp contrast between the housing available to the rich and the slums for the poor (left foreground).

Mass housing in the Soviet Union. It may not be very attractive to look at, but no-one ends up on the streets.

live, eat and sleep in the streets. The International Institute for Environment and Development estimates that in cities in developing countries, one person in three lives in overcrowded, rented slums. Their homes often have no piped water, drains, electricity or rubbish collection. European countries including the USSR, The Netherlands and West Germany claim they have no problems with homelessness. But although those countries may provide enough decent accommodation, the needs of their populations are changing (especially of young and single people), which means that many people do not have the sort of housing they would like.

In Britain, housing problems, including homelessness are set against a background of great social, economic and demographic (population) changes. In the early 1980s, there was a sharp rise in unemployment. For instance, in 1984 the building industry lost 400,000 construction jobs; and across the country the number of job opportunities for young people declined. In the past few decades significant changes in the population have intensified the pressure for additional new homes: people are leaving

7

The problems with housing are not new. Protesters march in London in 1962 to demand that the government requisition empty houses to provide homes for 1,000 families then in the care of the council.

their parents' home at a younger age, they are getting married later and households are smaller. In 1931, the average number of people in a household was 3.7; in 1986, the figure was estimated at 1.9. Tax cuts and a low rate of inflation mean that the majority of employed people in Britain are reasonably well-off. However, the substantial minority of about one-third of the population who are on low incomes such as the unemployed, disabled people, and pensioners who are to some extent reliant on state benefits, have not gained as much from the government's tax cuts. These are generally the same people who tend to live in unfit properties or become homeless.

Defining Homelessness

What does being homeless mean? The law has tried to define it, in the 1985 Housing Act, Part III (Housing the Homeless). This law was passed to ensure that certain priority groups—such as families—would not be forced to live on the streets, but that local authorities would have a duty to offer them permanent rehousing. The same law lays down a number of conditions a person applying as homeless must fulfil before being offered permanent rehousing.

Proving homelessness to gain a home
The first condition is that the applicant must be homeless. For instance, a person is defined as homeless if he has 'no accommodation which he and anyone else who resides with him as a member of his family ... is entitled to occupy; or if he has accommodation but cannot secure entry to it; or if there are threats of violence from someone residing with him'. In other words, to fulfil this condition the applicants must be able to prove they have nowhere to live.

If the local authority is satisfied that the applicant is homeless it will then consider the second condition: whether or not the applicant is in 'priority need'. Priority need covers those who are pregnant or have dependent

A sight becoming increasingly common on Britain's streets is that of homeless people trying to sleep, or begging from passers-by.

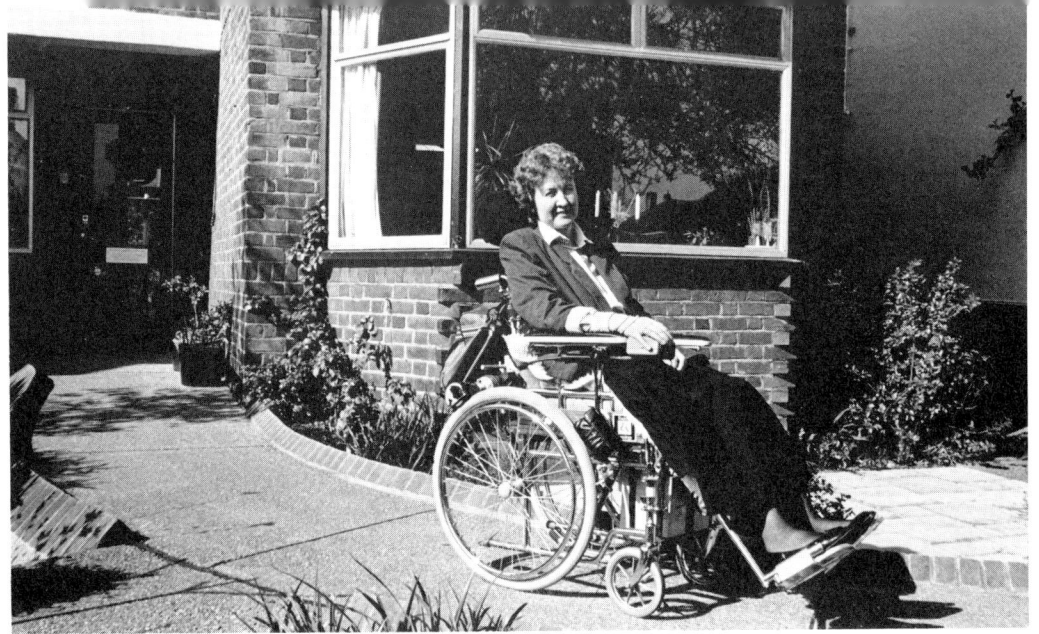

Under the 1985 Housing Act, some disabled people are considered to be in priority need to be rehoused because they would be vulnerable if they were made homeless.

children; people over retirement age; people who have a physical or learning disability such that if they were homeless they would be 'vulnerable' (for example, a blind or deaf person, or someone who is confined to a wheelchair). A person who has been subjected to threats of violence or actual violence within his or her own home is also considered to be in priority need. Some people may be considered to have a priority need for 'a special reason'; for example, some local authorities will consider all people aged 18 or under to have a priority need on age grounds.

Having satisfied itself that the applicant is homeless and in priority need, the local authority will then ask 'did the applicant become homeless intentionally?' The test of this is whether or not a person did something, or failed to do something, which resulted in the loss of his or her accommodation. For example, someone who gives up a council home to move to another area where he or she has found a job will normally be said to have become homeless intentionally, even though he or she had a good reason for moving. People who lose their home because of rent arrears will often be classed as intentionally homeless because they failed to sort out their financial affairs and save themselves from being evicted. This condition has caused more controversy than any other in the law on homelessness. Each year many people who are denied help by a local authority appeal to the courts to make the authority look again at their case. More cases come to court appealing against decisions on whether or not they are intentionally homeless than on any other part of the Housing Act.

Case Study 1:
Bill, aged 43

Bill is an alcoholic and sleeps rough in Liverpool. His wife threw him out three years ago after innumerable broken promises to give up drinking. He was sacked from his job on nightwatch after being found drunk in his hut while on duty. His few friends and family were unable or unwilling to help him and eventually they all lost touch with him.

Bill has been homeless ever since he was forced to leave his home, and now has no contact with his wife or children. As he says, 'Since then I've gone from bad to worse. Look at me, they'd be embarrassed by me now.' Bill spent his first few nights walking the streets. He went to the police, who suggested somewhere to try—a cheap local bed and breakfast hotel—'Hotel, they call it. Hardly any bedding. No heating. Never enough hot water, and the food's terrible.'

Bill also had problems trying to claim benefit from the Department of Social Security (DSS) while of 'no fixed abode'. For the first few months Bill did try to get a job, but 'No one really wanted to know. I was shunted from place to place.' He stayed in a DSS Resettlement Unit, which proved to be little better than any other shelter, '"The Spike" they used to call it. When you come in they give you a bath and take your clothes away. Then they give you handouts. You don't look like much and you don't feel like much ... but at least it's a roof over your head and three meals a day.' Gradually Bill became resigned to a life on the streets.

Most of the time Bill sleeps rough, anywhere sheltered. Inevitably, his health has suffered, 'I haven't stopped drinking, I suppose I don't really want to now. You have to fend for yourself. If you get wet you never dry out, and when it's cold, it's bound to make you ill. I can't get a doctor with no address.'

Bill doesn't feel that anyone has really tried to help him find a permanent home. Of the private 'hotel' he says, 'Sometimes you feel you're keeping them in a job, and some of them make a lot of money out of you, don't they? The DSS pays them, so they're all right.' He feels bleak about the future. 'I don't think there's much chance of me ever getting a home again. If someone said "Bill, I've found you a place", that'd be great, somewhere private with my own front door key. I still want that, but it won't happen, nobody cares enough.'

Many of the people who live on the streets end up as alcoholics, not least because alcohol dulls the pain when sleeping rough.

> 1. What sort of home do you think would be best for someone in Bill's position?
> 2. Should people be able to benefit financially from the predicament of Bill and others like him?
> 3. Do you think the law should require local authorities to house everyone, regardless of whether they are 'intentionally' homeless?
>
> Comment on this view, 'Everyone has the responsibility of housing themselves, the present law on homelessness simply encourages people to sponge off the state.'

Who are the Homeless?

In 1987, over 200,000 households applied as being homeless to local authorities. Of these, 103,000 were accepted as being homeless, in priority need, and not intentionally homeless. The remainder were refused help. Of the 200,000 households, 39 per cent had become homeless because friends and relatives could no longer accommodate them; marriage breakdown accounted for 19 per cent; 10 per cent had lost their homes through mortgage repossession (they were unable to pay for the loan on their house); a further 4 per cent because of rent arrears for their local authority or privately-rented accommodation; 23 per cent lost their local authority or privately-rented home for other reasons and 5 per cent had lost their job and the accommodation that went with it.

Out of the 103,000 accepted as homeless, 75 per cent were in priority need because of pregnancy or dependent children; 7 per cent were pensioners; 5 per cent were vulnerable due to a physical or learning disability; the remaining 13 per cent had a priority need for unspecified reasons.

A family put in temporary accommodation by the local council. In 1988 over 27,000 families were being housed temporarily by councils.

This is a bedroom in a London bed and breakfast hotel that was taken over by Camden Council. The owners had been charging £80 a week for people to live in what was classed as a 'double' room.

Being rehoused
What happens to people accepted by a local authority for permanent rehousing? They will rarely be offered permanent accommodation immediately. Homeless people in London must often wait for up to two years in some form of temporary accommodation which may be a bed and breakfast hotel, a hostel or a short-life flat (see glossary).

Bed and breakfast hotels have been called the slums of the 1980s. Overcrowded conditions and inadequate facilities have led to deaths in fires. Health visitors believe there are links between inadequate bed and breakfast accommodation and children being underweight, prone to ill-health and having behavioural problems. Marriage breakdown while in these hotels is common, possibly as a result of the tensions of living in such conditions.

In June 1987, there were 33,870 homeless households in bed and breakfast hotels or other forms of temporary accommodation in Britain.

The annual cost of housing one family in bed and breakfast accommodation in a non-metropolitan area is £5,475, and in London it is £10,900. The annual cost of providing a family with a council house in a non-metropolitan area would be an estimated £3,700, and in London £7,000.

The annual amount spent on paying for temporary accommodation by local authorities in England and Wales was £32,177,019 in 1987. It might be worth considering how many permanent local authority homes could be built for these huge amounts.

Not eligible for rehousing
What happens to those people refused rehousing by local authorities under the 1985 Act? Their only right is to 'advice and assistance' from the local authority in finding somewhere to live. People who might be considered as vulnerable—such as alcoholics or drug addicts—are often not considered by local authorities as in priority need. This is because local authorities claim that their vulnerability is in large part a matter of choice—they have made themselves vulnerable by their addiction to drugs or alcohol. Such people are forced to live in accommodation like emergency nightshelters, which provide a roof, but little else in terms of support. They cannot gain access to council accommodation. So, some people feel that there should be housing schemes to provide clean, warm, secure accommodation for those in such a position, and support when necessary to sort out other areas of their lives.

The charity Homeless Action provides cheap short- and medium-term housing in London (like this shared house) for women of all ages.

A mother and her child in a Gingerbread hostel. Although the hostels offer some refuge, in time the strain of being homeless takes its toll.

There are further implications to consider in cases where local authorities do not help families with permanent rehousing. If such families fail to find alternative rehousing, they may have to split up. In 1984, some 830 children were taken into care because their parents were homeless. So there may well be other costs to set against the financial ones of providing families with permanent rehousing.

In Britain in 1988, there were an estimated 350,000 single homeless people living in squats, lodgings, hostels and bed and breakfast hotels. There were many more single people living unhappily at home because they did not have enough money to move out and live independently. Single homeless people are rarely rehoused by local authorities. Those depending on social security benefits or on low incomes find it very difficult to secure privately-rented accommodation and impossible to take out a mortgage. At present neither the government nor local authorities see such people as in need of priority rehousing aid. Another body of opinion holds that single people or intentionally homeless people have a right to help with their rehousing. Central government gives financial help to people buying their own homes; but the private rented sector is declining fast, and fewer local authority homes are being built—so some argue that those who lose out because of this policy ought to be treated better (see chapter four). Often it is the pressure of poor housing that encourages people to turn to drugs, such as alcohol, to help them cope.

Case Study 2:
Mary, aged 22

Mary and her fifteen-month-old son Harry, live in a hostel run by Gingerbread, the organization for single parents. Harry is 3 kg underweight and Mary is ill, she has a stomach ulcer, and her nerves are in shreds.

Mary and her husband bought a house when they married, and both worked full-time to pay off the mortgage from their building society. 'We were just getting by,' she says. 'We were working all the hours God sent and yet we still didn't have enough money once Harry was born. There was a lot of strain. Mike worked shifts and I worked evenings and weekends for extra money ... but I was living on my nerves.'

The couple struggled on, trying to meet payments on the mortgage and hire purchase loans they owed for the furniture. Then, when Harry was four months old, Mary found she was pregnant again. Her husband wanted her to stop working, but Mary knew they couldn't afford it. 'We just couldn't exist on his wages. There really was no way that I could stop working. I desperately wanted to keep the house, and I felt that the longer I went on working, the better chance we had of coping.' But Mary became ill, had to stop working, and the couple began to get behind with their mortgage payments.

Mary thought the only sensible thing to do would be to give up their home and try to rent somewhere cheaper, rather than risk the house being repossessed by the building society. 'This hurt my husband. He'd worked so hard to give us a nice home. He'd spent all his free time working on the house and there I was saying we should leave it, that he couldn't provide for his family,' says Mary.

When the house was sold, the money just paid their debts. The local council refused to help. They said the family were intentionally homeless. They should have waited for the house to be repossessed and then applied for rehousing. Mary went to live with her parents, and had a miscarriage. Her husband couldn't forgive her for giving up their house and left her.

Desperate to leave her parents' home, Mary contacted Gingerbread, who had a room free in their hostel. A housing association has offered help with rehousing, and Mary hopes that her husband will return once she has a home for him.

A bed in a shelter may be the only home available to many young people who have travelled to London in search of work.

1. Should banks and building societies be allowed to repossess a home if people suffer a drop in income or lose their job?
2. Do you think that homelessness is the result of other social problems or the cause of them?
3. What advice would you have given Mary?
4. Given a limited supply of housing, who would you rehouse first?

Housing in the UK

Many people become homeless either because there is no suitable accommodation available, or because they do not have the money to rent or buy that which is available. The problems with housing lie at the heart of the homelessness crisis.

During the twentieth century, owner-occupation has increased dramatically (see page 6); private tenants make up only a small part of the population; the remainder of non-owners are tenants of local authorities and housing associations. The present situation has arisen through policies which see owner-occupation as the preferred form of housing for most people. Since the 1960s, governments have encouraged home ownership by giving financial incentives to home buyers. Governments have believed that helping people to become owner-occupiers will reduce the amount of money needed to build local authority homes, and so reduce public expenditure on housing. No other area of government spending has been cut as much as that on public housing (over 50 per cent) since 1979.

A former council house (right) that has been bought by its tenant. The sale of council houses has meant that in 1988 there were about 74,000 fewer council homes available to let than in 1980.

With a decreasing housing stock and government incentives for home buyers, house prices, especially in the South, have risen fast.

Owner-occupation

Most people cannot afford to buy a house outright. They therefore arrange to take out a loan, called a mortgage, from a bank or a building society. The loan is repaid over a number of years agreed between lender and borrower. Mortgage interest tax relief is an allowance made to somebody who is repaying a mortgage. In effect, it means that they pay less income tax than otherwise. The amount of tax relief allowed by the government to owner-occupiers (on up to £30,000 of their mortgage) rose from £1,145 million in 1979–1980 to £3,500 million in 1984–1985, an increase of 300 per cent. The rate of mortgage interest tax relief allowed increases with the amount of tax paid, so those highly taxed on high incomes receive higher relief. Because of this, mortgage interest tax relief helps people on low incomes least—the same people who are most likely to become homeless.

Mortgage interest tax relief is available to people who are employed. If they lose their job, unemployed owner-occupiers must wait six months before the DSS pays the full cost of the interest on their mortgage (they get no financial help with paying off the principal part of the mortgage, that is, the amount of money borrowed). The six-month delay puts their repayments further into arrears and they come under threat of losing their homes. Building societies and banks will often treat sympathetically people who cannot pay their mortgage because of job-loss. Nevertheless, 54,754 owner-occupiers were taken to court in 1984 for arrears in repayments; of these, 35,397 had their homes repossessed by the mortgage-lender, leaving them homeless. In 1979, 10,950 mortgages were over six months in arrears; in 1984, the figure was 50,150.

An eviction in progress. Once evicted, it can be very hard for people who are on low incomes, or unemployed, to be rehoused, especially if their council considers them 'intentionally' homeless.

An area of increasing concern is the issue of disrepair in owner-occupied homes. Two groups of people are particularly affected by this: the elderly and those on low incomes. A large proportion of both these groups live in properties built before 1919. The government's House Conditions survey of 1981 said that out of all dwellings in serious disrepair (needing repairs estimated at £7,000 or more) 49 per cent were occupied by elderly people. Sixty-two per cent had heads of households who were not in full-time work and therefore dependent on a part-time job, a pension or social security benefits. Those in such circumstances may find difficulty in meeting the costs of repairing their properties. Improvement grants are obtainable, although the money available for grants has been reduced. The number of homes improved through grants in 1984 was 320,000; in 1985 the figure was 196,000.

It may well be true that most people want to own the place in which they live, but there are pitfalls. Would-be purchasers need to consider what would happen if they became unemployed; if they needed to move to another part of the country; or if they had no money to carry out essential repairs. Becoming home owners does not necessarily protect people from becoming homeless.

In 1988, elderly people in Portsmouth received free repairs to their homes from the 'Care and Repair' scheme. Care and Repair is a charity that carries out this kind of work on a regular basis.

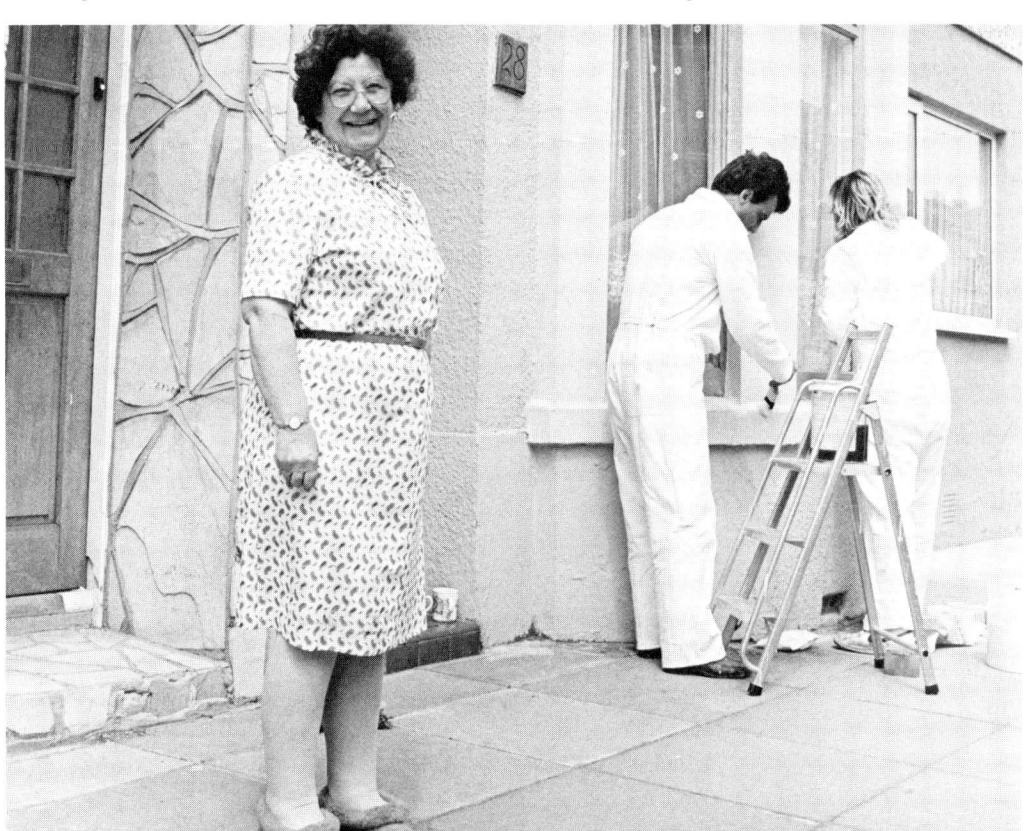

Councils are stuck with system-built blocks of flats, many of which are now considered unsatisfactory. Ronan Point showed the flaws in its design when a corner of it collapsed after a gas explosion (1968).

Renting from a local authority

The next major form of house tenure in Britain is renting from a local authority. As far back as the 1920s governments have swung between investing heavily in public housing and making substantial cuts. The number of local authority homes built in England and Wales in 1982 was 32,600; back in 1974 it was 156,000.

The effects of policy changes are also felt in the deterioration of local authorities' existing housing stock. In 1985, the Audit Commission said that such stock in England and Wales would take £900 million to repair.

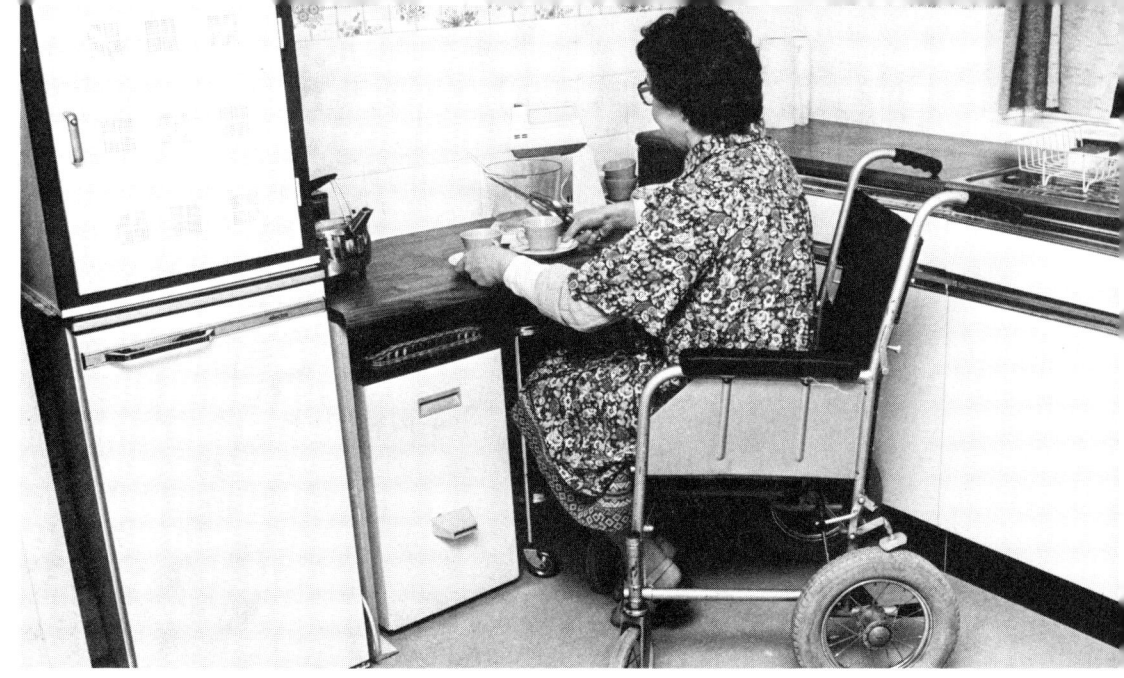

Sheltered housing for the elderly and disabled includes features like low-level surfaces, making it easier to cope with daily chores.

Local authorities have inherited a legacy of system-built dwellings, such as tower blocks, which make up about 5 per cent of all dwellings owned by local authorities. In addition to problems of rapid disrepair, some feel that these produce unattractive environments and that their design is unsuited to most families' needs.

However, only 1.3 per cent of local authority housing stock is considered unfit, compared with 18 per cent in the private rented sector and 4.7 per cent of owner-occupied stock. Essential repairs are the responsibility of the local authority. Mobility schemes enable council tenants to transfer to council accommodation in other parts of the country. Local authorities provide 350,600 sheltered accommodation units for the elderly and for people with special needs, such as physical disability.

Local authorities are often criticized for the number of their properties that are allowed to stand unoccupied. There are approximately 27,500 vacant council properties. However, this should be compared with the 94,000 vacant private houses. On the whole, council housing provides secure, relatively cheap accommodation for millions of people.

Renting from a private landlord

Most of Britain's worst housing conditions are found in privately-rented homes: 13.5 per cent of these lack one or more of the basic amenities (toilet, bathroom, hot and cold water), as opposed to 3.3 per cent of owner-occupied dwellings and 2.8 per cent of local authority properties.

There are far fewer houses and flats available to rent today than in the past because landlords can make more money by buying and selling property than by renting it out. Apart from being in short supply, privately-rented properties tend to be in a worse state of repair than owner-occupied properties, because landlords are often unwilling to spend money on improving property that is rented out since they will not be able to get a quick return on their investment.

The people most likely to be private tenants are the elderly, single people and childless couples on low incomes. The 1,200,000 people on council house waiting lists to some extent reflect the number of people living in unsatisfactory private rented accommodation who want to move to a council rented dwelling.

The steep decline in the number of private properties available to rent means that this type of accommodation is often no longer an option for home-seekers. As a result there has been criticism of the rent control system which, it is said, discourages landlords from renting. Rent control involves the level of a tenant's rent being set by a neutral public official. Others defend rent controls, arguing that without them rents would gradually rise, using up a larger and larger proportion of tenants' incomes.

Private tenants frequently suffer from poor housing conditions. Often, landlords themselves are unable to pay for improvements.

People may also be discouraged from renting out rooms or property by a belief that once a tenant is in the accommodation, a landlord can never get rid of them. In fact this is not the case. If a landlord can prove in court that the tenant has deliberately not paid rent, or is acting in an 'untenant-like' manner, the court can order the tenant to be evicted. The principle behind the law affecting a tenant's rights to 'security of tenure' is that a landlord cannot evict a tenant for no good reason: the landlord will have to prove the case against a tenant in court, and the decision to evict the tenant is made by a county court judge, not the landlord.

Housing associations and housing co-operatives
An increasing amount of reasonably-priced accommodation is provided by housing associations and co-operatives. Housing associations are non-profit organizations and charge fair rents to their tenants. They often work together with local authorities on joint schemes to house those in need. They are usually run by a committee of local people and receive grants from central government.

One of the buildings run by the Two Piers Housing Co-operative in Brighton. Built in 1987, this co-operative houses 40 people.

Derelict housing is wasted housing. Pressure groups have urged the government to take steps to reduce the amount of vacant property.

Housing co-ops are usually buildings divided into flats which are managed or owned by the residents. The residents carry out the duties that the landlord would normally be responsible for, such as repairs and maintenance. If tenants have bought themselves into the co-op they may take a share of the profit when they leave. Housing co-ops receive government funds and have to show that they have put this money to good use.

Paying for rented accommodation
Both council tenants and private tenants who are on low incomes can claim housing benefit to meet up to the full amount of their rent and 80 per cent of their rates. The amount of housing benefit each claimant can receive depends on his or her income. If they are unemployed they will get the full benefit. People working for a low income can have a proportion of their rent and rates paid. In 1988, a total of 5,010,000 families received some level of housing benefit.

We can see from this brief survey of the present housing situation in Britain that a substantial majority of the population are adequately housed. However, many of the rest are in low-standard accommodation, trapped by their low income in housing which is often in disrepair, with inadequate facilities. It is this section of the population and the homeless who seem to need more from the government's housing policies.

Case Study 3:
Maggie, aged 78

Maggie lives on her own in a country village in the cottage she has lived in for the last 52 years. She owns the cottage and only pays rates and electricity bills.

The cottage is cold and damp, the only source of heat is the old kitchen stove, which burns coal and as much wood as Maggie is able to collect. Maggie looks around, 'I can't do as much as I used to, since my husband died it's not so easy to keep it all up.' A draught blows in around the ill-fitting door, and sodden pieces of fabric and paper are fixed around the edges of windows with rusty drawing pins. There is a damp mouldy patch, where the plaster has come away, under one of the windows.

As well as being depressed by the state of the house and worried about its effect on her health, Maggie finds herself increasingly isolated. 'People have been gradually moving away from the village—the only newcomers to the area are those who've bought holiday homes. They live in London most of the time and there's simply no chance of getting to know them.

'The village is more than a mile away (1.6 km), with just one shop left, and the nearest post office is another six miles (9.7 km) on the bus. It takes all day to get my pension, and it is hard bringing all my shopping back. People are helpful, with their cars and that, getting me things, but I don't like to ask.

'About a year and a half ago, I finally decided to sell the cottage and move into a warm, comfortable flat. But the cottage has been on the market for a year now, the price has been knocked down twice, and no one is interested in buying. Unfortunately the cottage needs a tremendous amount of work doing to it, but if the price goes any lower it'll not be worth selling, and there's no way that I'd have enough to pay for a decent modern place.

'So I'm stuck here—I've no family to go to. It's funny, I'd always thought that once the mortgage was paid, I'd be safe and sound. ... I've been told that I could apply for an improvement grant from the council—but I'm too old to start re-decorating now; I think that the money would be better spent on a young couple starting a new home. For the time being I'm just going to cross my fingers and hope that someone comes along soon to buy the cottage.'

The need for sheltered housing for the elderly is likely to increase in years to come, yet demand already exceeds supply.

1 What kind of help would you want if you were in Maggie's position?
2 Do you think Maggie deserves to be rehoused?
3 Do you think it is a good idea for the government to spend money on helping people to repair their own homes?
4 Do you agree with government money being 'spent' on mortgage interest tax relief? Where else should the government spend money on housing?

Young and Homeless

As we have already seen, young single people are the 'hidden' homeless. If they are 17 or over, if they have no children, are not pregnant or do not have a physical disability or a learning disability they will not be considered to be in 'priority need'. They are entitled only to advice and assistance from the local authority in trying to find somewhere to live.

Moving out
There are no official statistics for the numbers of young people who move away from home each year. Some have arranged a place to go to, but others leave without planning ahead and so may well find themselves homeless. Scarcity of rented accommodation, high rents, long council house waiting lists, high unemployment and low wages all make it difficult for young people to find a place in which to live.

Many people leave their family home between the ages of 16 and 24 as part of the natural process of growing up. But there may be other reasons.

Flat hunting—young people leaving home stand a much better chance of finding a place to live if they stay in their home town.

London, June, 1988. An unemployed, homeless girl sits begging near Charing Cross station. If she is over 17 and left her previous home voluntarily, the local authority is not obliged to house her.

A broken home, conflict or tensions in the family, violence or overcrowding may force young people—some of them under the age of 16—to leave home before they are ready. Young lesbians and gay men may be forced to leave home when their parents become aware of their sexual orientation. All these young people risk becoming involved in drug abuse, prostitution, or crime; many may then come to the attention of the police. Some may be lucky enough to find a job and accommodation. Others are forced to return 'home' or, if under the age of 17, they may be put into local authority care. Perhaps they may be helped by one of the appropriate voluntary organizations.

The problem is not primarily that young people leave home: but that when they do, there is no housing available specifically for them. There is virtually no local authority rented housing available to young single people, who are competing with better-paid adults for private rented accommodation. Young black people may also encounter discrimination.

At 16, anyone can legally leave home, but people under the age of 17, can be put in 'a place of safety'—for example a social services home—if the police have reason to believe that they are in 'physical or moral danger'. People under 18 are still legally in the 'custody, care or control' of their parents or guardians—unless they are in care of the local authority, wards of court, or married.

Finding a home

Buying a house or flat is expensive and it can be difficult to find accommodation to rent in most parts of the country. A look through any local newspaper will show you how expensive it is. Some employers may provide accommodation with a job, and colleges have personnel to help with information about finding accommodation. Young people can claim income support and housing benefit if they have no other source of income.

The housing options most commonly available to young single people include: houses, flats, bed-sitting rooms, hotels and lodgings, hostels, squats and short-life housing, emergency shelters or sleeping rough.

Houses are expensive to buy and rent. A young person leaving home is unlikely to be able to afford to buy a house, but in some cases may be able to rent one. A group of people might share a rented house: by paying a share of the rent, each can afford to live in it.

A flat is usually self-contained with its own kitchen and bathroom. A large flat is also expensive to buy or rent, but again it is possible to share a flat in the same way as a house.

A bed-sitting room, or bed-sit, has a bed and space for sitting in. Sometimes it has its own cooking and washing facilities, and sometimes a shared kitchen, with a shared bathroom and toilet.

Bed and breakfast hotel accommodation might be considered by young people leaving home until they can find somewhere more permanent. However, if the person is on income support, the DSS will only pay a fixed amount for a limited period for bed and breakfast. In 1988 the maximum the DSS would pay in London was £48.30 per week. If bed and breakfast owners are assured of this level of payment, and constant demand from young people, they will have no incentive to ensure that their hotels are of a decent standard. There is nothing in law to prevent them from making up to three or four people share one room. People aged 25 or under are also subject to time limits on their benefit. In some south coast areas, the DSS will pay a person's bed and breakfast charge for two weeks only; after that they must move out of the area to continue receiving their payments. In London, the board and lodging charge is paid for eight weeks before young people must move on. Time limits do not apply to those on a training scheme or attending a rehabilitation programme.

Inside a London squat. Many of the people who end up squatting have gone to London from the North in search of work. At times there have been as many as fifteen people living in this one-room flat.

Hostels are usually run by non-commercial organizations. They provide sleeping accommodation, shared washing and toilet facilities, and sometimes cooking facilities or meals. There is short-term accommodation—such as that provided by the Youth Hostels Association for holidaymakers—and emergency overnight accommodation for people who would otherwise be sleeping rough. Long-term accommodation is provided by college authorities, or voluntary organizations such as the Young Men's Christian Association (YMCA) and Young Women's Christian Association (YWCA).

Squatters gather their belongings after being evicted from the Stamford Hill Estate in London in 1988. Most of them had nowhere else to go.

Each Christmas, from 23 to 28 December, Crisis at Christmas opens a shelter in central London. Anyone can come to the shelter, which provides beds, three hot meals a day, help from doctors, chiropodists and hairdressers, and a change of clothes. Crisis at Christmas works year-round to raise funds for the shelter and for permanent hostels.

A squat is empty accommodation that is taken over by a person or group of people to live in. It is legal to squat in an empty building, provided it is not broken into (it must be possible simply to walk into it), and it is not required as a dwelling by the owner. However, the owner can have squatters evicted by getting a court order. To provide short-life housing, organized groups such as housing associations and housing co-operatives may manage empty properties awaiting redevelopment. By agreeing to collect rents to use for maintenance such groups can provide more security and better living conditions than is usually available in squats.

Emergency shelters are provided by voluntary organizations for people who would otherwise be sleeping rough. They are often housed in large halls or similar buildings and give basic bed and shelter for a night.

Sleeping rough means sleeping wherever a space can be found to lie down. That includes: pavements, parks, abandoned cars, bus shelters, and so on. However, this is not necessarily free: a Shelter worker reports that in 1988 gangs were charging rent for a sleeping space on the Embankment in London.

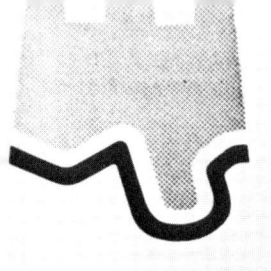

LONDON BOROUGH OF TOWER HAMLETS
DIRECTORATE OF HOUSING
PO BOX 62, 255-279 CAMBRIDGE HEATH ROAD
LONDON E2 0HQ

Dear Sir or Madam,

HOUSING BENEFIT – ASSISTANCE WITH RENT AND RATES   28/10/87

From 28/9/87 you will not have to pay so much rent. Because you are receiving Supplementary Benefit you have been granted Housing Benefit of £487·64 per week which will be deducted from your rent. Details of your new char (if any) will be sent to you shortly. The reduced charge should be paid on the due dates on your rent vouchers. If ther is NIL to pay and your rent account is clear, then you do not need to make any payments. If you are in arrears with yo rent, then you must make arrangements with the Rent Arrears Section to pay the money you owe.

£6·83 to pay per week for heating & hot water

IMPORTANT

Councils are paying private hoteliers huge sums in order to house people temporarily. In 1988, in London alone, the bill for bed and breakfast accommodation came to over £100 million.

Someone claiming income support who has found a flat, bed-sit or hostel place can claim housing benefit from the local authority to meet all the rent and 80 per cent of the rates. A person must claim from the date they move into the accommodation, so they do not accumulate any arrears. Someone who has found a place in a bed and breakfast hotel should go to the DSS on the day they move in, and claim the board and lodging payment. If working, they may be entitled to housing benefit to meet part of the rent and rates. It is worth making a claim as more people are entitled to housing benefit than is generally thought. However, bed and breakfast is a very expensive option for people on low incomes as they are entitled to housing benefit on only a very small proportion of the board and lodging charge. Anyone thinking of taking such accommodation should find out exactly how much rent they will be charged before moving in.

It is hard to find somewhere to live at short notice, but homeless people often have more success if they try their home town. Here they are on the spot and can respond quickly to advertisements in local newspapers. Places to rent are snapped up quickly. Helpful friends and contacts may also hear of places 'on the grapevine'. Whatever the situation, it is always better to plan ahead before moving out of home, by making sure there is somewhere else to go to at an affordable price. The nearest Housing Aid Centre, Citizens Advice Bureau or other such agency will give advice.

Case Study 4:
Rose, aged 19

Rose is living in a squat in London. She left her family and her home in Manchester two months ago because she couldn't find a job there. Her parents are also unemployed and were struggling to look after their four children. Being the eldest child, Rose felt that the only option was to seek work in the South and send money home.

'The first thing I did when I got down here was look for a job. It was incredible, I got a job as a shop assistant in a department store on my first day. Since then I also got a job in a pub. But, as it turned out, finding a job was not the real problem.

'I couldn't believe it when I looked through the papers for a place to live, the rents are ridiculous—£60 a week for a room in a shared house! Everywhere I went, people wanted a month's rent in advance and a deposit, which often meant more than £300. I couldn't get a loan for the money, I didn't even have a bank account; there was no way that I could get that much together without months of saving up.

'Luckily, a few friends from school had come down to London before me, so I stayed with them for a while. One of them told me about a friend of hers who was living in a squat, there was room there and that's where I live now.

'The squat's cold and dirty, there's no electricity or even running water. But at the moment we're trying to get it classed as short-life housing, which would allow us to have the basic amenities.

'I don't like it in the squat; as soon as I can afford it I'll move into something a bit better. But for the moment it's the only real alternative to sleeping on the streets, especially if I'm going to send any money home, which was the whole point of me coming to London.'

1 Rose would almost certainly not be considered in priority need to be housed if she applied to the local authority, but do you think she has a right to be housed?
2 Should people who have had to move to a new place in search of work be treated differently to other people who are classed as intentionally homeless?

What do you think of this opinion: 'People who leave a perfectly good home in search of the bright lights of a city, deserve to end up homeless, the same applies to drunkards and drug addicts'?

How much money should the government put forward to help people maintain their properties? These houses, built at the same time, have obviously not been equally well kept!

Tackling Homelessness

In Britain at present there appears to be no common agreement on what homeless people are entitled to in the way of housing, or even what their needs are. Without such an agreement it is difficult to argue for a set of housing rights.

We know that a substantial proportion of the population is either homeless or living in accommodation that is unsatisfactory for one reason or another. If we accept that this is a problem which needs the attention of the government, then we need to look for agreement on what people have a right to expect from their housing circumstances. Some feel that all people are entitled to accommodation suitable to their needs—a home they can call their own whether it is their own room, flat or house; the accommodation should be in an acceptable state of fitness, having the five basic amenities—toilet, bathroom, washbasin, and hot and cold water.

New council housing in the London Borough of Islington. Housing has improved as councils have learned lessons from the 1960s.

Nicholas Ridley, Secretary of State for the Environment, believes that the 'pressures of the market' will solve the housing crisis.

We could also look beyond the physical environment and say that people's wishes need to be taken into account: do they want to buy their own home or rent from the council; where do they want to live; what type of accommodation do they prefer? However, there needs to be a general will to acknowledge that such needs are in fact housing *rights* in order for a government to form policies that will respond to these needs.

In November, 1988, a new Housing Act was passed. The Conservative government that put it through felt that the most urgent housing need was for more privately-rented accommodation. The Act is intended to provide this by changing the regulations that bind private landlords in a way that will encourage people to rent out housing. However, some people, including Shelter, have criticized the Act because it makes no provision for building new homes, and fear that the lack of regulation on landlords may mean higher rents, less security for tenants and ultimately more homelessness. The Conservative Government feels that enough new housing will be supplied by private developers. Those who oppose them believe that an adequate supply of private housing will be met only at a price that people on low incomes cannot afford to pay.

The chair of Shelter, Lord Pitt (far left) joins the director of Shelter Sheila McKechnie (far right) at the launch of Shelter's 'Housing Britain—Let's Get to Work' Campaign. Helping them sign up is the cast of the television series Auf Wiedersehen Pet.

A still from the 1966 BBC TV play Cathy Come Home. *The play focused on the way in which homelessness caused families to split up. Over 20 years later homelessness is still a major problem.*

Shelter, the national campaign for the homeless, has launched a Housing Rights Campaign to build support for its central aim: a decent home for everyone at a price they can afford. Various actions that the government should take have been suggested. These include:

a) releasing more money for building new homes and repairing and improving existing dwellings (including making more improvement grants to home-owners)
b) reviewing the way public money is allocated for housing, with greatest provision going to those in greatest need
c) restricting mortgage interest relief to the basic rate of tax
d) running council housing on a non-profit basis
e) introducing legislation to give a framework of housing rights, setting minimum standards and giving security and control of housing
f) encouraging local authorities to build more homes
g) making more money available to housing associations to provide more rented accommodation at prices people can afford
h) making more provision for groups most at risk from homelessness—the old, the young, single-parent families, women, the disabled and ethnic minorities.

The Housing Rights Campaign is an alliance of local and national groups involved with housing and the homeless. It campaigns for the legal right to a safe and satisfactory home for every member of the community, in the same way that there is a right to health care. The campaign has recently demanded that the government provide the money to build the new homes that are needed and to improve the older ones, in consultation with the people who will live in them.

The campaign has drafted a Housing Rights Act that it would like to see made law. The Act would have provisions for setting standards on housing, space, insulation and state of repair. It would require housing authorities to rehouse all people made homeless because of unfit property; help disabled people to adapt their homes, or have them rehoused in suitable accommodation; and provide a home for everybody who needs one. There would be powers to take over empty homes, and new controls over holiday homes.

To tackle homelessness hard decisions have to be made. For example, since large sums of money will be needed, should the money come from individuals, from the government, or from both? Decisions about housing provision can be made at a national level, at local government level, or at a community level, as can the decisions about design, construction, and management. But the basic decision which remains to be taken is whether or not housing is a right that should be available to everyone who needs it. Only when agreement is reached on this question will the problem of homelessness be tackled effectively.

Specially converted temporary accommodation is provided for the single homeless by Hackney Council as a planned alternative to paying for bed and breakfast accommodation for the homeless.

1. What, in your opinion, makes a house into a home?
2. How important do you think housing is compared with, say, defence or national health?
3. What sort of place do you live in? Is it suitable for you? Does it need repairs? Is it basically comfortable and clean? Would you like to live somewhere else?

Useful Addresses

Alone in London Service, 188 King's Cross Road, London WC1X 9DE (01-278 4224) (Advice on accommodation in London for homeless people up to the age of 21.)

Campaign For Single Homeless (CHAR), 5-15 Cromer Street, London WC1H 8LS (01-833 2071)

Children's Legal Centre, 20 Compton Terrace, London N1 2UN (01-359 6251) (Helps under 18 year olds.)

Empty Property Unit, 88 Old Street, London EC1V 9HU (01-233 0202) (Advice on how to set up a short-life housing group.)

Federation of Black Housing Organisations, 374 Grays Inn Road, London WC1X (01-837 8288)

First Key, Hartley House, Green Walk, London SE1 (01-378 7441) (For those leaving care.)

Gingerbread, 35 Wellington Street, London WC2E 7BN (01-240 0953) (A self-help group for single parents and their children.)

National Association of Citizens Advice Bureaux, Myddleton House, 115/123 Pentonville Road, London N1 (01-833 2181) (Will tell you where your nearest Citizens Advice Bureau is.)

National Federation of Housing Associations, 175 Grays Inn Road, London WC1 (01-278 6571) (Will put you in touch with local housing associations and co-ops.)

Shelter Housing Aid, 88 Old Street, London EC1V 9HU (01-233 0202) (Has a national network of advice agencies. For Wales contact Welsh Housing Aid, 57 Walter Road, Swansea (0792-469400).)

YMCA (Young Men's Christian Association), 640 Forest Road, London E17 (01-520 5599) (Has hostels around the country for men.)

YWCA (Young Women's Christian Association), 2 Weymouth Street, London W1 (01-580 6011) (Has hostels around the country for women.)

Glossary

Asthma A breathing disorder that can make it difficult for a person to breathe.

Audit Commission The commission audits (inspects) the accounts of local authorities and other public bodies in England and Wales. It was set up in 1983 to ensure that public services provided value for money.

Co-operative An organization owned and run equally by its members.

DSS (The Department of Social Security) This government department oversees welfare payments such as supplementary benefit.

Environment All the conditions that surround living things. A person's home environment is important because he or she spends so much time there.

Financial incentive Money used as a reward to encourage people to do something. Mortgage interest tax relief acts as a financial incentive for people to buy houses, by reducing the amount of tax they have to pay.

Gay Homosexual. Many homosexuals prefer to use this term to describe their sexuality.

Hire-purchase A way of buying goods that cost a lot of money (such as a car), in instalments. You can use the goods after paying a relatively small amount as a deposit, but you only own the goods when you have paid the last instalment.

Housing benefit The money paid by local authorities to people on low incomes, to pay for some or all of their rent and up to 80 per cent of their rates.

Inflation A situation where there is a rise in prices and the cost of living in general.

Lesbian A homosexual woman.

Local authority In Britain, the governing body of a county, district or town. It is made up of councillors who are democratically elected. Housing is one of the main responsibilities of local authorities.

Metropolitan Relating to a large city (a metropolis) and its suburbs. In the UK, districts like Greater London and Greater Manchester are metropolitan.

Mortgage A promise that a property will be given over if a loan is not repaid. When people want a loan to pay for a house, the house is mortgaged as security.

Public expenditure The money spent by government—for example on building houses.

Short-life housing Property owned by a local authority or a housing association that is vacant for some reason (usually because it is awaiting redevelopment) and has been allowed to be occupied temporarily by people who agree to look after it.

Squat (Verb) To occupy a house or a piece of land without the permission of the owner. (Noun) Housing in which people are squatting.

Tenant Someone who occupies a room, flat, house or any property. To be classed as a tenant under the law, a person must have exclusive possession of the property, he or she must pay rent for it and must be contracted to stay for a certain period.

Tenure The holding or occupying of a piece of property such as a house or flat.

Further Reading

Benefits: CHAR's guide to income support and housing benefit for single people without a permanent home (CHAR, 1988)

Filling the Empties, by Ross Fraser (Empty Property Unit, 1986)

Finding a Place to Live in London, (Housing Advice Switchboard, 1986)

Homes For Single People, (Available free from the Scottish Council for Single Homeless.)

Housing and the Law, by Gwyneth Vorhaus (Wayland, 1986)

Housing Rights Guide, by Geoff Randall (SHAC, 1986)

Leaving Home in the News, by Dorothy Turner (Wayland, 1983)

School Leavers Handbook, (Adamson Books, 1986)

Squatters Handbook, (Advisory Service for Squatters, 1986)

The Rent Acts and You, Wanting to Move? Shared Ownership (How to Become A Home Owner in Stages), (Dept. of the Environment, Welsh Office, 1986). (Available free from libraries, Citizens Advice Bureaux, and housing advice centres.)

Acknowledgements

The publishers would like to thank the following for providing the illustrations in this book: BBC 42; Camera Press *front cover*, 6, 7, 20, 30, 35, 40; Format Photographers 31 (Ingrid Gavshon), 14 (Pam Isherwood), 21, 34, 39 (Jenny Matthews), 27, 44 (Maggie Murray), 10 (Joanne O'Brien), 13 (Raissi Page), 5, 15, 22, 24, 29 (Brenda Prince); Network Photographers 33 (Mike Abrams), 19 (Laurie Sparham); Mark Power 4, 12; Shelter 16 (James A Gardiner), 41 (Brenda Prince), 36 (Andrew Wiard); Topham 8, 23; Wayland 25 (Michael Marchant), 9, 18 (Chris Schwarz), 26, 38 (Paul Seheult).

Index

bed and breakfast hotels 11, 14, 16, 32, 33, 36
bedsits 32, 33, 35
benefit claims 11, 16, 27, 32, 33, 35, 36

charities 4
  Crisis at Christmas 4
  Homeless Action 15
  Shelter 4, 42
council houses 5, 10, 14, 15, 16, 19, 23, 24, 25, 31, 40, 42
council house waiting list 25, 30

disabled people 4, 8, 10, 13, 24, 30, 42, 43
DSS 11, 21, 33, 36
DSS Resettlement Units 11

emergency nightshelters 15, 32, 34, 35
eviction 10, 26, 35

flats 25, 27, 32, 33, 35, 39

government housing policies 16, 27, 43

home improvements 5, 22, 25, 27–9, 35, 42, 43
home ownership 6, 19–25
hostels 14, 16, 17, 32, 34, 35
housing
  associations 17, 19, 20, 27, 35, 42
  authorities 43
  conditions 5, 6, 8, 14, 16, 22, 24, 25, 27, 39
  co-operatives 26–7, 35
Housing Act
  (1985) 9–10
  (1988) 41
Housing Rights Campaign 43

intentional homelessness 10, 12, 13, 16, 17

International Year of Shelter for the Homeless (1987) 4

landlords 24, 25, 26
local authority care 16, 31
lodgings 16, 32

mobility schemes 24
mortgage interest tax relief 20, 21, 29, 42
mortgages 13, 17, 20–21, 28

pensioners 4, 8, 13, 22, 24, 25
permanent rehousing 9, 14, 16
  priority need applicants 9, 10, 13, 15, 16, 30
private tenants 19, 25
privately-rented accommodation 5, 13, 16, 24, 25, 31

rent
  arrears 10, 13, 21, 36
  control 25, 35, 37
renting from local authorities 19, 23, 24, 40

sheltered accommodation units 24
short-life housing 14, 32, 34, 35, 36
single parents 17, 42
sleeping rough 11, 32, 34, 35, 36
squats 16, 32, 35, 36
state benefits 8, 22, 35

temporary accommodation 14, 15, 34
tenants 19, 24, 25, 26, 27
  rights 24, 26

unemployment 7, 8, 21, 27, 30, 36

voluntary organizations 31, 34, 35, 45
  Gingerbread 17, 45

young homeless 30–31